ANDALUSIAN LANDSCAPE

Tim Gartside

SANTANA
BOOKS

Published in Spain by Ediciones Santana S.L.,
Apartado 422,
26940 Fuengirola, Málaga, Spain.
Telephone (95) 248 5838. Fax (95) 248 5367.
e-mail santana@vnet.es

Printed in Spain by Gráficas San Pancracio S.L.,
Poligono Industrial San Luis, Calle Orotava 17, Málaga.
Depósito Legal: MA-1.089/1997. ISBN: 84 - 89954 - 00 - 3

DEDICATION

For my Parents, Grandparents and Yvonne
for all their support.

ANDALUSIAN LANDSCAPES

Andalusia is the land of cliches. Whisper its name and the romantic in us conjures up vivid images of brave toreros strutting across the sand, dark-eyed gipsies exploding into passionate dance, blood-red geraniums spilling from balconies in white-washed villages, and the sensous sound of guitar music drifting through jasmine-scented patios on summer nights.

It is also the land of superlatives. It is the largest, most southern and, many say, the most beautiful of Spain's 17 regions. Within its 87,000 square kilometres, an area larger than Austria or Ireland, are the highest mountains in mainland Spain and the highest village in Europe.

Andalusia produces the best bullfighters and flamenco artists, and has some of the country's biggest and most colourful fiestas. It's towns and monuments - Granada and its Alhambra, Cordoba and its Mosque, Seville and its old Santa Cruz quarter - are world famous.

Along its Atlantic coastline, stretching from Gibraltar to the Portuguese border, shimmers a string of dazzling white fishing towns including the sun-bleached capital Cádiz, believed to be the oldest seaport in western Europe, and wind-swept Tarifa, Europe's number one spot for surfers.

Sitting at the crossroads where Europe meets Africa and where the narrow Gibraltar Strait provides a routeway for thousands of migrating birds, Andalusia is a wildlife paradise. Nearby is the incomparable Coto Doñana, Europe's foremost wetland reserve, which attracts wildlife lovers from all over the world.

As if all these superlatives were not enough, Andalusia has the best climate and mildest winters in Europe, which is why tens of thousands of foreigners have settled along its Mediterranean shore stretching westwards from Malaga to Gibraltar, the sunshine coast known throughout the world as the Costa del Sol, without doubt the favourite retirement area for northern Europeans.

Mingling with the summer crowds in the smart resort towns along the Costa del Sol, it is hard to imagine that just a few miles inland you can explore mountainside villages where time has stood still and the locals still ride to their fields on mules and donkeys.

More than anything, Andalusia is a land of contrasts. In no time at all you can drive from semi desert in the east to marsh lands in the west, from crowded or quiet beaches in the south up through rolling farmland and broad river valleys to dense forests and high mountain ranges in the north.

It was to this region that Tim Gartside came to live in the late eighties. At first the young Englishman trod the beaten path of a million other photographers, furiously clicking away at all the famous sights and monuments and countless colourful fiestas and ferias, but more and more he was drawn deeper into the countryside .

Tirelessly and with a sharp eye, he captured through his lens the charm of remote villages and lonely farmhouses, fields ablaze with sunflowers and meadows full of poppies, the play of light on olive groves and the sun rising and setting over the high sierras.

Before returning to London, where he now lives and works, Tim Gartside had amassed a huge library of photographs, a selection of which is published in this book as a celebration of the astonishing collage of colours and textures to be seen in the landscapes of Andalusia.

Previous page: Poppies in a wheat field near Morón de la Frontera, Seville.

San Cristobal peak overlooking the mountain village of Grazalema, Cádiz.

A lone campo house in the majestic mountains of Ronda, Málaga.

The Serranía de Ronda, littered with boulders, has often the air of having been laid waste by armies of vengeful giants.
                                        —Ted Walker.

Above: An ancient tower in an olive field near Yunquera, Málaga.

Right: A partial view of Benadalid, one of many pretty pueblos in Málaga province.

*There lies the first of her villages,
down in the river hollow, with a fine
old bridge to take you there...In you go,
down the whitewashed cobbled streets,
and all around you seem to be flowers.*
— Jan Morris.

Farm land outside the town of Ronda, Málaga.

Previous page: A field of sunflowers in a farm near Córdoba.

*Andalusia is romantic Spain,
popularised by Gautier, Merimée,
Bizet and Washington Irving,
and still dangerously bewitching.*
— Jan Morris.

An old olive tree shades an abandoned farm house near Algodonales, Cádiz.

Above: Dusk descends on the hilltop village of Olvera, Cádiz.

Right: Fields of sunflowers are a familiar sight in the Andalusian countryside.

Previous page: Sunset over the mountains near Mijas, Málaga.

Perhaps the most beautiful view in the world...
row upon row of desert hills, carved and shaped by wind and
water, and covered with olives and little bushes of almond trees.
— Gerald Brenan.

A well-kept finca in fertile farm land near Pinos Puente, Granada.

An abandoned farmhouse in a ploughed field near Ronda, Málaga.

I looked back at the broken ranges running to the sea,
at the naked dark trunks of cork oak stripped of bark,
at fields of gorse with limestone jutting out...
— Ernest Hemingway

Above: Young olive trees on a farm near Antequera, Málaga.

Right: A field ablaze with wildflowers near El Gastor, Cádiz.

Previous page: A hill covered with olive trees near Villanueva del Rosario, Málaga.

Above: A well-preserved hermitage beneath the ruins of a hilltop fortress in Cártama, Málaga.

Left: A yucca in lone splendour in the Sierra de Aljibe, Cádiz.

Beyond the Sierra Morena
lies the land of promise,
golden Andalusia,
tilted towards the sun.
           - -Laurie Lee

Above: Poppies in a wheat field near Pizarra, Málaga.

Left: Olive trees in a ploughed field near Arriate, Málaga.

Thick bouquets of green leaves and golden-centred, rose-coloured flowers between the crevices of grey limestone rocks...one of the most exhilarating spectacles that the aesthetic botanist can get in Europe.
— Gerald Brenan.

Above and right: Mist and mountains above the village of Grazalema, Cádiz.

Andalusia is indeed a land of contrasts.
— Michael Jacobs.

Above: The sun sets on the Mediterranean coast at Mijas-Costa, Málaga.

Left: A lone farmhouse in the countryside near Ronda, Málaga.

The track led over undulating farmland with the great mountains bounding the southern horizon. I do not think I have ever seen a more beautiful landscape, even in Kashmir.
— Penelope Chetwode.

Above: A field ready for planting on the road from Málaga to Granada.

Left: The breathtaking gorge dividing the town of Ronda, Málaga.

Looking down from the Ronda cliff across the plain on a still and translucent October day, poised somewhere in the sunlight between earth and sky with late-migrating swifts arrowing over the roofs and the call of bells drifting up from the village below, was to be as close to heaven as anyone can reasonably require.

—Nicholas Luard.

Above: The sun-scorched Sierra de las Nieves in summer.

Right: A quiet and cooling beach near Fuengirola on the Costa del Sol.

Previous page: Dawn breaks as a Málaga fishing boat heads into harbour.

Nothing can give you any idea of these great Spanish plains which seem to have been deserted since the dawn of creation.
— Alexandre Dumas.

Above: Poppies in a wheat field near Coin, Málaga.

Left: A mountain stream in the Alpujarras, Granada.

*A week ago I walked about 45 miles and climbed about 12,000 feet
to see streams rushing out of caves of snow on to green meadows.*
—*Gerald Brenan.*

Above: Storks nest in a ruin on the road from Sevilla to Mérida.

Left: A working farm in the countryside near Ronda, Málaga.

Above: Olive trees in a wheat field near Coin, Málaga.

Left: A mountain stream in the Serrania de Ronda, Málaga.

The extraordinary beauty of their countryside made me
feel that I had ridden through the garden of Eden before the Fall.
— Penelope Chetwode.

Above: An orange grove in the Mijas valley, Málaga.

Right: Dawn silhouettes the Moorish-style Castillo Bil Bil at Benalmádena-Costa, Málaga.

Previous page:: The picturesque mountainside village of Gaucín, Málaga.

A farmhouse surrounded by olive trees in the Serrania de Ronda, Málaga.

Outcrops of rock dominate the landscape in the Sierra de Montehacho, Málaga.

Most of her vast landscapes have still never felt the tread of a tractor ... All still feels ordered and graceful, the energies of the earth rising through ear of corn or trunk of olive into the walls and crowning towers of the villages, sprouting like outcrops of rock from the soil.

— Jan Morris.

Rows of sun beds await the tourists as dawn breaks on the Costa del Sol.

To awake early and watch the sun rise from the glowing sea
is one of the many joys of living by Andalusia's Mediterranean shore.

- Aubrey Marks.

Above: Poppies in a wheat field near Morón de la Frontera, Sevilla.

Left: A cork tree in a ploughed field near Jimena de la Frontera, Cádiz.

Only a faint hazy bloom of dull green from the olives and almonds mantled the fierce red earth...The Andalusian austerity offered maximum contrast to the soft and soggy England we had left behind.
— Hugh Seymore-Davies.

Above: Gently sloping green fields near Cártama, Málaga.

Left: A field full of wildflowers high up in Las Alpujarras, Granada.

Springtime in the Alpujarras is magical,
with the olives and almond blossom
giving off a very sweet, delicate odour.
—Barbara Lloyd.

Above: The picturesque mountain village of Benadalid, Málaga.

Right: A classic Andalusian farmhouse near Ronda la Vieja, Málaga.

Previous page: The snow-capped Torrecillas peak in the Sierra de las Nieves.

Andalusia is a land of contrasts where ancient pueblos cling to barren mountain sides and look down on fertile, stream-fed valleys far below.
— Aubrey Marks.

Lingering snow high up in the Sierra Nevada, Granada.

Oak trees in the countryside near Zahara de la Sierra, Cádiz

Land of the exploits of the Homeric heroes,
of the Phoenician settlements, of the first Greek colonies,
of the last stronghold of the Moors. One does not
enter Andalusia without a leaping of the heart.
— Rose Macaulay.

Above: A blazing field of sunflowers in the countryside near Córdoba.

Left: A lone cork tree surrounded by golden wheat in the Coin valley, Málaga.

This is Córdoba's Campiña region ... in spring and early summer a blazing yellow carpet of sunflowers and dark-green foliage, interspersed with the lighter green of ripening wheat.
— David Baird.

Above: Rows of olive trees stretching to the distant hills of the Serrania de Ronda, Málaga.

Right: A church tower peeps above the palms in the nature park near El Bosque, Cádiz.

Previous page: A Moorish fortress crowns the picture-postcard pueblo of Casares, Málaga, said to be one of the most photographed villages in Spain.

Above: A wide-spreading oak in a field near Algodonales, Cádiz.

Previous page: The fabulous Alhambra Palace in Granada.

Walled towns and villages built like eagles' nests
among the cliffs...ruined watchtowers perched on lofty peaks.
— Washington Irving.

A watchtower overlooking the Olvera valley, Cádiz.

For a free catalogue of our books
on Spain dealing with travel, food, history,
gardening, nature, language and law
please write to:
Santana Books, Apartado 422,
29640 Fuengirola (Málaga) Spain.
Telephone (95) 248 5838. Fax (95) 248 5367.
E-mail: santana@vnet.es